PAPIER MÂCHÉ

PAPIER MÂCHÉ

Juliet Bawden

Photography by Carl Warner

CONRAN OCTOPUS

To Steve and Jill

First published in 1996 by

Conran Octopus Limited, 37 Shelton Street, London WC2H 9HN

Text copyright © Juliet Bawden 1996

Papier mâché designs copyright © Madeleine Adams, Gerry Copp, Jacqueline Shelton, Melanie Williams 1996

Design and layout copyright © Conran Octopus 1996

Photography copyright © Carl Warner 1996

Illustrations copyright © Emily Hare 1996

Art Editor: Alison Fenton

Commissioning Editor: Louise Simpson

Project Editor: Alison Bolus

Production Controller: Mano Mylvaganam

Illustrator: Emily Hare

Template Illustrators: Chris and Elly King

British Library Cataloguing in Publication Data

A catalogue record for this book is available from the British Library

The right of Juliet Bawden to be identified as Author of this Work has
been asserted by her in accordance with the Copyright, Designs and Patent Act 1988.

ISBN 1 85029 682 0

Typeset by Richard Proctor

Printed and bound in Hong Kong

Produced by Mandarin Offset

CONTENTS

Introduction

Papier mâché is a craft form with a long history which has become extremely popular in the last 10 years. There are a number of reasons for this. It is very inexpensive and easy to do and, stylistically, it must be one of the most diverse mediums around. It can be done in the home and the scale of the pieces ranges from the smallest item of jewellery to large pieces of sculpture or even furniture. It is also environmentally friendly because of its emphasis on recycling.

Since my first book on papier mâché was published in 1990 there has been a plethora of books on the subject. What makes this one distinctive is the conviction of its editor, Louise Simpson, that although beginners require projects that are relatively easy to make, this does not mean that they should be offered projects devoid of any artistic merit. The fact that they are beginners does not mean that they do not have a discerning eye and a desire to create works of a high standard. With this in mind we selected four of today's top papier mâché makers whose work offers a fascinating variety of construction and decorative techniques. I hope you will feel sufficiently inspired by the high standard of work in this book to create some of the projects for yourself or to try some of the variations shown.

TOP LEFT *Small household items such as frames are a popular choice for papier mâché. They can be used for mirrors or pictures, and can be constructed from both pulp and paper layers. The work shown here is typical of this artist's work, being very brightly coloured with a simple pattern of suns, flowers and birds.* (MADELEINE ADAMS)

TOP RIGHT *It may look like a relic or find from an archaelogical dig but this urn is constructed from papier mâché layers round a balloon, with template-cut handles attached to the sides. The finish on the urn is what gives it its aged appearance. It is a favourite combination with this artist, involving rubbed-in oil pastel, worked over with gold gouache to produce a broken surface.* (JACQUELINE SHELTON)

BOTTOM LEFT *At first it may seem a little strange to make jugs from papier mâché since the finished items will not be watertight, but they can be used for displaying dry items such as pencils, paper or papier mâché flowers, or simply hung from a shelf for a pretty display. The style of these jugs, and their decoration, is unashamedly cottagey, as is much of this artist's work.* (MELANIE WILLIAMS)

BOTTOM RIGHT *As this jaunty looking bird proves only too well, papier mâché does not have to have any function at all – it can be pure whimsy. It is items such as this that are great to turn to when you are at a loss as to what to give for a distinctive birthday or Christmas present. The decoration relies heavily on torn paper shapes, which are a dominant feature of this artist's work.* (GERRY COPP)

Tools

1   Washing-up bowl
2   Developing tray (as alternative to 1)
3   A4 tracing paper pad
4-6 Pen; Pencil; Chinagraph pencil
7   A3 sheet of tracing paper
8/9 Mixing palette and small dish
10 Protective gloves
11 Sieve
12 Hacksaw
13 Liquidizer
14 Glass bowl
15 Icing bag and nozzle
16 Cocktail sticks
17 Needle
18 Rubber
19 Craft knife
20 Pliers
21 Wire cutters
22 Scalpel
23 Pair of compasses
24 5 cm/2 in paintbrush
25 1 cm/½ in paintbrush
26 Artists' paintbrushes
27 Sandpaper
28 Glass jar
29 Scissors
30 Petroleum jelly
31 Cling film/saran wrap
32 Ruler

Materials

1   Coloured tissue papers
2   Satin varnish
3   White emulsion paint
4   Sheet of hardboard
5   Applicator for 11
6/7 Sheet of mirror and 2.5 cm/1 in square
8   Goldsize
9   Masking tape
10 Crayons
11 Tile cement
12 Coloured cartridge papers
13 Paper clips
14 Brooch findings
15 Wire and enamelled wire

16 Silver leaf
17 Toilet tissue
18 Chicken wire
19 Balsa block
20 Collage items
21 Clock mechanism and hands
22 Two-part epoxy resin
23 Gold leaf
24 Plain flour
25 Sand
26 Coloured embroidery thread
27 Mount card
28 Oil pastels
29 Liquid gold leaf

30/31 Gold and coloured gouaches
32 Wallpaper paste
33 Newspaper
34 Coloured foils
35 Magnets
36 Balloons
37 Poster paints
38 Spray fixative
39 Spray varnish
40 White spirit/turps substitute
41 White household glue (PVA)
42/43 Interior wall filler/ready-mixed
44 Cardboard tubing
45 Thin dowelling (instead of kebab sticks)

Layering Papers

YOU WILL NEED

MATERIALS
Newspaper · plain flour (a large cupful) · water · (wallpaper paste or white household glue/PVA can be used)

TOOLS
Balloon · bowl for paste · fork · bowl for balloon · thread for hanging

THE TECHNIQUE of modelling papier mâché over an inflated balloon is a well-known one. The balloon is inflated to the desired size, before being covered with strips of paper and glue. When the layers of papier mâché have hardened, the balloon is burst and removed to leave a bowl shape. Spouts, handles, lips or rims can then be added to this shape.

1 Make the paste by adding water to the flour or wallpaper paste, beating continuously to prevent lumps forming until the paste is the consistency of batter. Make only the amount of flour and water paste you need as it does not keep. Glue should be diluted 50:50 with water.

2 Blow up the balloon to the size you desire the finished object to be. To keep the balloon steady, place it in a bowl to prevent the balloon turning on to its heaviest side, as the paper is applied. Rip the paper into 2.5 cm/1 in x 7.5 cm/3 in strips down the grain. The first layer of papier mâché is applied with the glue on both sides of the paper, smeared on by hand or paintbrush. Overlap the pieces of paper as you work. Complete 2 layers, then hang it to dry in a warm place. Apply 2-3 more layers.
N.B. If glue is used, all 5 layers can be applied before the work is left to dry.

When layering strips on to anything other than a balloon, treat the mould with a releasing agent such as petroleum jelly or cling film, and do not use paste or glue on the first layer.

NEWSPAPER immediately springs to mind for making papier mâché, but there are masses of other papers available with their own characteristics and qualities. A strong brown wrapping paper is good for construction, a flimsy tissue paper is better used for decoration. Below we show you some examples used with a variety of glues and pastes.

Newspaper with flour and water paste

Inexpensive and easily available, newsprint is the most popular paper used for papier mâché. It can vary in strength, in general the broad sheets using better quality paper. Flour and water paste is environmentally sound, and when dry can be sanded to a smooth wood-like finish.

Typing paper with diluted glue

Here at last is a use for all those old letters and circulars. Old typing paper is best used white side out, as this will save having to prime it later on with emulsion. White household glue is versatile and quick-drying and may be diluted or used at full strength.

Photocopy paper with wallpaper paste

This is a very inexpensive glue, and a little goes a long way. The best way to apply this glue is to dip the ripped pieces of paper into it and then wipe off the excess between the thumb and forefinger. Photocopy paper is easily available but may need more coats to achieve the same thickness and strength of stronger papers.

Sugar paper with flour and water paste

Sugar paper is a thick heavy paper often used for pulp work as the fibres break down easily. It can be dyed and cut or torn into shapes to create the finish on a piece of work. Used here with flour and water paste it gives a surface which is softer in quality than newspaper papier mâché.

Crêpe paper with diluted glue

Crêpe paper responds well to creasing (froissage) and can be used to create texture in a piece of work. As can be seen in the example here, it looks interesting layered and has a translucent quality which can be used to good effect creating new colours when layered together.

Brown paper with wallpaper paste

Brown paper is very good for creating larger pieces of work, as is any paper with long fibres, such as blotting paper. If you are modelling figures, brown paper makes excellent raincoat material, canvas or even leather. Wallpaper paste has added fungicide to prevent it from forming mould as the papier mâché dries.

Tissue paper with wallpaper paste

Tissue paper is a versatile decorating material. It is especially useful for covering chicken wire armatures, drying to a tight skin. Colour contrasts can be exploited by using pieces of overlapping tissue paper. Its elasticity makes it useful for filling and it will squash up easily into nodules or bumps.

BELOW (from left to right) dish – brown paper with wallpaper paste; small jug – newspaper with flour and water paste; eggcup – tissue paper with wallpaper paste; plate – sugar paper with flour and water paste; large jug – photocopy paper with wallpaper paste; cup – crêpe paper with diluted glue; basin – typing paper with diluted glue.

Making and Using Pulp

PULPED PAPIER MÂCHÉ is – quite literally – 'mashed paper': a soft clay-like material that can be manipulated into shape and dried. The advantage of using pulp over the layering technique is that there is only one stage of the process, and although it takes longer to dry, it is very sturdy, especially if a filler has been added. Pulp is also highly suitable for sculpting and moulding, and ideal for small intricate objects and fine detail. It tends to be thicker and have a more organic look than layered papier mâché.

YOU WILL NEED

MATERIALS

Paper · water · white household glue

TOOLS

Bowl · liquidizer · sieve · washing-up bowl · cling film/saran wrap or petroleum jelly

1 The most basic pulp can be made by filling a bowl with paper torn into small squares, covering the paper with warm water, and leaving it to soak for 24 hours. If you wish to make a coloured pulp, as here, use coloured sugar paper. Each colour can be made in a separate batch and stored in individual plastic bags or other air-tight containers. If you wish to

decorate the pulp by painting, then use any un-dyed paper such as typing paper or newsprint. If you use newspapers, the printing will make the pulp grey, but this can be overcome by painting a base coat of white emulsion on to the finished item.

Add the pieces of soft wet paper a few at a time to the liquidizer, which should be at least half full of water. Switch the liquidizer on for a few seconds at a time and then stop it. This will prevent the motor burning out. Repeat this process until you have a wet pulpy mixture.

2 Strain the pulp through a fine sieve, extracting as much water as you can by pushing the pulp with the back of a spoon or the palm of your hand. What you want is a mixture that you can mould and form into shapes and that is not too wet, because the glue has yet to be added. Tip your strained pulp into a large bowl, such as a washing-up bowl. Repeat the process until you have enough mixture to fill the bowl. (If you are starting with just a small project, then make less.)

3 When you have sufficient pulp for your purpose, start adding the glue, mixing it into the pulp gradually until the

A collection of bowls made from pulped papier mâché. The papers vary from brown wrapping paper to turquoise sugar paper and purple tissue paper. The addition of flower petals and sawdust lends texture and colour.

pulp feels like soft clay. Your pulp is now ready to use for your first project.

(A more advanced method is to boil the paper and water mixture – which has already been soaking for 24 hours – for 20 minutes, before sieving off the excess water and adding the adhesive.)

4 Cover whatever you are using as a mould with cling film/wrap or petroleum jelly. This will stop the pulp sticking to the mould as it dries. Picking up a little at a time, push the pulp on to the mould to make a layer about 1 cm/½ in deep. Make sure all the pieces are joined together. Leave the mould to dry in a warm place where air is circulating. You will know your piece is dry when it is hard to the touch, and sounds hollow when tapped. Your piece is now ready to ease away from the mould.

You can vary the texture and strength of pulp by using different papers and adding different fillers. Newsprint and typing paper make a good workable pulp, but if you want a finer pulp, which dries to a porcelain-type finish, use tissue paper. Different fillers can be used to add weight, such as chalk or cellulose filler, or to add texture, such as sawdust.

Using Moulds

ALMOST ANY papier mâché construction you make will need a mould as a base. Some moulds are removable, such as the bowl and the jug shown here, and the balloon on p.10; others become an integral part of the object itself (see the template and armature examples opposite).

When using a removable mould, always remember to treat any mould other than a balloon with a releasing agent (see right), or you may find that the mould isn't removable after all.

Once you have mastered layering on to existing moulds, experiment with templates and armatures to create more unusually shaped objects.

SIMPLE MOULDS

1 Smear the outside of the bowl with petroleum jelly or cover it with cling film/saran wrap before applying your first layer of paper strips (see Layering, p.10). Once your papier mâché is completely dry, gently twist it off the mould. If the paper shape gets stuck when you try to remove it, you may have to cut a little away with a craft knife and repair it with a couple of layers of paper once the object is released.

The same method can be used for any shape, provided it is possible to remove the papier mâché form from the existing mould without damaging either.

COMPLEX MOULDS

2 If you choose to model around something from which it will be impossible to remove the papier mâché in one piece (such as the shaped jug Melanie used for her Country Jug, see p.70), you will have to cut the papier mâché version in half with a scalpel (being very careful not to damage the original mould). You may need to slide a knife in between the mould and the papier mâché in order to remove it. Reassemble the piece then cover it all with 2 layers of paper to hide the join and make it whole once more.

TEMPLATES

3 Templates made out of cardboard will remain incorporated in the final papier mâché product. Small-scale templates, such as Madeleine's fish (shown here), Melanie's animals (see p.62) or Gerry's brooch (see p.80), can be quickly covered in layers or pulp and then decorated. Use of larger-scale templates, such as Madeleine's mirror frame (see p.32) may involve building and sculpting pulp to just some areas (in this case the border). Templates are an excellent way of translating favourite images into papier mâché constructions. You will find the designs needed for the projects in this book on pp.I-XII.

ARMATURES

4 Armatures are very useful for creating unusual or intricate shapes that would not be feasible without the integral support the armature provides for the papier mâché. One of the strongest and most flexible materials appropriate for an armature is chicken wire (as shown here), although all sorts of materials can be used, including wood, coat hangers or other wire (see Melanie's flowers on p.66).

Wear thick protective gloves when moulding chicken wire, snipping off unwanted pieces with tin snips. When you are satisfied with the shape you have created, cover it in one layer of tightly stretched tissue paper, before applying pulp or further layers of strips.

Adding Embellishments

AS WELL AS considering the visual impact that additional protrusions are going to make on a piece, it is essential to remember that, particularly in the case of handles and spouts, they must be sturdy and practical too. It is pointless spending hours on the body of a jug only to find that the handle falls off the first time it is picked up; so follow the instructions carefully. Done correctly, the join will not prove to be the Achilles' heel of the piece; it will also be invisible after being sanded and painted.

NECKS AND LIPS

1 This method of constructing a neck involves building up two sets of strips of paper, both placed vertically, one inside the urn and the other outside. The strips support themselves to form a neck. The same technique can be used to form a lip, though in this case the strips should be bent to an angle of 45 degrees.

An alternative method of forming a neck is to cut a strip of card and bend it into a ring, then attach it with masking tape. Cover the card and the join with layers of paper and allow it to dry thoroughly.

HANDLES

2 Trace the handles from the templates provided in this book (pp.V and VI), or draw your own straight on to some strong card. Cut out your shapes using a craft knife, working on a cutting mat, then tape them in place with masking tape. Cover the entire piece, including the handles, with 3 layers of paper strips. Leave to dry.

An alternative method is to form a handle from wire and pierce both ends through a papier mâché piece, before covering the handle and join with paper pulp or layers (see Melanie's Country Jug on p.72).

RIMS

3 The easiest way to form a rim is to cut one out of card and attach it to the bowl (or other object) in question. In this case Gerry has traced round her papier mâché bowl to get the inner dimension of the rim, then drawn on her pointed rim. (The rim shape is provided on p.XII for your use.) Once the rim has been cut out with scissors or a craft knife it should fit snugly on to the bowl. Since this is a pulp bowl, the join between rim and bowl was neatened with pulp pressed into the crack. A layered piece would have strips passing over the join.

FEET

4 These sturdy feet are made from balsa wood sawn into blocks, shaved with a craft knife and then smoothed with sandpaper into approximate spheres. Before being attached with glue they will be decorated with gold leaf to match the Musical Box they support. Such balsa spheres also make good handles.

Another way to make feet would be to mould pulp into spheres (no larger than 2 cm/¾ in in diameter) and leave them to dry thoroughly, before decorating them and attaching them to the object.

Decoration

THE MATERIALS WITH which papier mâché may be decorated are infinite. The four artists in this book use a range of decorative techniques from gilding, distressing and painting, adding ripped paper and collage pieces, and even applying interior wall filler using an icing bag. You will see many examples of their techniques throughout this book. The surface upon which you decorate will also affect the finished look of the item. For example, a priming layer of gesso, instead of the more usual – and more economical – white emulsion, gives papier mâché a ceramic-like finish.

INTERIOR WALL FILLER

Interior wall filler is an easy way to add a three-dimensional design to a surface. It is best to mix the filler yourself to obtain the correct consistency, which should be slightly runnier than the ready-mixed variety. It is applied by putting it into an icing bag with fitted nozzle and squeezing it on to the surface. Once the plaster design has been applied, leave it to dry for at least an hour. Then brush a layer of diluted glue (50:50 with water) over the relief design to adhere it to the surface and prevent it from dropping off. The glue will also act as a form of protective varnish.

GILDING

Gilding is the application of metal leaf over a coat of glue or goldsize that is almost but not quite dry. The metal leaf comes in sheet form, as real gold and silver leaf, or fake gold, sometimes known as Dutch gold or schlag, and fake silver, which is in fact aluminium. The fake metal leaf is usually attached to a backing paper (and is sometimes known as 'transfer metal leaf'). It can be cut into shapes and applied quite easily by placing the metal face-down on the surface, rubbing on the back, then taking away the backing paper. A gentle rub over the leaf with a soft dry brush ensures adhesion. Real leaf is more expensive and can be harder to use, but it does offer a more random effect.

COLLAGE

Collage comes from the French word coller, meaning to stick. It is the term given to a picture or pattern built up from pieces of paper, cloth or other materials stuck on to a surface. Jacqueline Shelton uses collage to great effect, sticking pieces of musical score, stamps, tickets and small stones and shells on to her papier mâché pieces, thus adding texture as well as decorative interest. It is also the ideal way to personalize pieces. Torn paper can also be collaged to great effect, as Gerry Copp shows in her work. See overleaf for more detail and a close-up example.

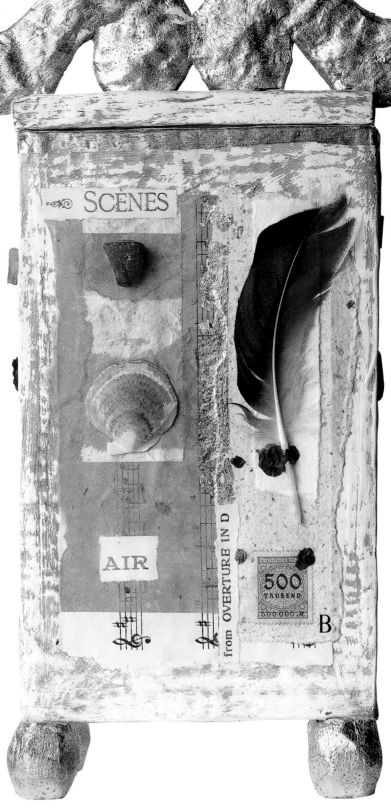

TORN PAPER

Tearing paper looks straightforward, but there is a knack to achieving your desired effects. To tear long, thin strips, with fairly smooth edges, you need to tear along the grain of the paper; for rough-edged pieces, tear across. To tear circles is a little more difficult and takes practice. It helps to draw a circle on the back of the paper and to tear round this, using the line as a guide, especially if you want a number of circles the same size. Use this same technique for other geometrics.

DISTRESSING

This term is applied to paint techniques where two or more colours are painted on top of one another and then rubbed with sandpaper so that the colour or colours beneath are revealed in a patched or distressed-looking way.

The jug shown here was first sanded smooth and then painted with layers of white, pink and blue emulsion (with drying times allowed between each coat). The surface of the jug was then gently rubbed to reveal the various colours hidden beneath.

PAINT SPATTERING

When well done, spattering will make a fine mist of paint dots, adding subtlety to a painted surface. It can be messy, so either cover all surrounding surfaces or make a spattering booth by placing the object in a cardboard box to contain the flying drops of paint. The best brush to use is a hard-bristled one. Load the brush with some paint, hold the bristles back with your finger, then let go. The further your brush is from your surface the finer the mist will be.

PAINTED DESIGN

Draw your design on in pencil first, either freehand or traced, and then paint using these guidelines.

Your choice of brush is important. Have a medium to large brush for the background and some very fine brushes for the detailed work. It is also important not to put too much paint on to the brush, with the inherent risk of flooding a small area. If you do make a mistake, leave it to dry and then paint over it with white emulsion. Once this is dry, you can draw and paint the design once more.

COLOURS OF THE SUN

A LARGE SERVING BOWL decorated with golden yellow sunflowers set in a sea of Prussian blue is the ideal vessel for serving fruit or bread at a summer lunch party. The accompanying table napkin rings are decorated with stylized stars in rich hues of warm terracotta and turquoise highlighted with flashes of gold.

Immediately one is attracted by the bold use of colour, but it is the hidden depths, achieved by the use of layers of gouache and crayon, which have lasting appeal. After the paint is applied the bowl is finished with a layer of matt non-toxic varnish both inside and out to protect it and make it suitable to hold food.

ABOVE *Surely the most dramatic and evocative of all summer flowers, the sunflower makes a striking decorative image.*

Stripy Fish Magnets

FISH HAVE RECENTLY become very popular as a visual expression in arts and crafts, and seen here they make charming magnets. It is their combination of bright, often unusual colours and a relatively simple body shape that makes them so appealing, and this simplicity also makes them an excellent first project on which to develop your skills.

YOU WILL NEED

MATERIALS

Cardboard · paper pulp (see Techniques, p.12) · newspaper strips · white household glue · white emulsion · gouache colours · spray fixative · clear satin varnish · two-part epoxy resin · small magnets

TOOLS

Pencil · tracing paper · templates from p.l · scissors · bowl · plastic spatula · 1 cm/½ in paintbrush · palette · artists' paintbrushes

1 Trace the templates from p.l or copy fish shapes from illustrations in books or magazines. Using a pencil so that you can rub out any mistakes, draw the fish shapes onto card, then cut them out.

To build up the fish bodies, take small amounts of pulp and press them gently on to the top of the card shapes, contouring them as you work so that the middle of each fish is fatter than the edges or fins. Make sure the pulp areas are joined together and then smooth the surface with a plastic spatula or with your hands. Leave to dry for two days, or until completely dry (the time will vary depending on the thickness of the pulp and the warmth of the room).

An ideal drying place is an airing cupboard, particularly in cooler weather when room temperatures will not be very warm.

2 When the pulp is completely dry, cover it with a layer of papier mâché strips (this is to provide a smooth surface on which to paint). To do this, take some small strips of newspaper and, using your fingers, smear them with a 50:50 mixture of glue and water. Then apply the strips to the top of the pulp, overlapping each piece slightly as you work, and smoothing out any air bubbles that appear. When the whole of the top of the fish is covered, leave it to dry, and then turn it over and cover the cardboard underside with further strips. Leave this to dry.

3 Coat each fish back and front with 2 coats of white emulsion, leaving drying time in between coats. The emulsion not only covers the newspaper and stops the type showing through, but it also acts as a sealer. (An alternative to emulsion for this purpose is acrylic gesso; this produces a thicker coat than emulsion and can be sanded down to a mirror-smooth surface.)

4 Decorate each fish with designer's gouache (or, if you prefer, acrylic or poster paints). As you can see, the colours Madeleine has chosen are quite subtle and the pattern a simple stripe. Note how the stripes curve round the contours of the fish body to give a more naturalistic look. You may prefer your fish to have tropical colouring with flashes of blue and yellow or streaks of turquoise and purple. Again, use books for reference or go to your local pet shop to look at real fish.

To make your fish ready for use, wait until all the paint is dry, then spray with fixative to seal the design. Brush with 2 coats of varnish, and, when this is dry, use a small amount of epoxy resin to stick a magnet on the back of each one.

Alternatively, if you would rather make them into a mobile, pierce a hole through a suitable point in each fish with a darning needle and suspend them to 'swim' in the air.

Mexican Mirror

BY LOOKING AT THE work of this artist it is easy to see that she is an optimist. The colours sing out at you, and the striking designs have a confident air.

The frame is simplicity itself to make, and yet, as with all Madeleine's work, the result looks very professional. The frame is made by building up a pulp border on a hardboard-backed mirror, and then covering this with paper strips to give a smooth surface. The designs are painted on to the white background, and then the surrounding colour is filled in.

The frame in the reflection is decorated with Roman numerals and stars, making a delightful contrast with the Mexican suns and fan-tailed birds on the larger mirror.

There is no reason to restrict yourself to square or oblong mirrors. The fish design shown right encircles a round mirror space; it also has a much wider border than do the two mirrors shown left. Vary your basic shape, border size and decoration to achieve the effect you want.

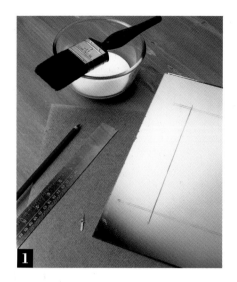

YOU WILL NEED

MATERIALS

*Sheet of mirror, 33 x 33 cm/13 x 13 in ·
2 picture hooks or rings · sheet of
hardboard, 33 x 33 cm/13 x 13 in ·
white household glue · tile cement ·
paper pulp · newspaper strips · white
emulsion · gouache colours · spray
fixative · clear satin varnish*

TOOLS

*Chinagraph pencil · ruler · bradawl ·
5 cm/2 in brush · ribbed spatula (comes
with tile cement) · bowls · greaseproof
paper · large paper scissors · 1 cm/½ in
brush · tracing paper · pencil ·
templates on p.II · artists' palette ·
artists' paintbrush · clear acrylic varnish*

1 Mirrors, like glass, comes in different
thicknesses and weights, and it is
worth taking advice from your local glass
merchant as to which is best for your
mirror frame. You may wish to make a
shaped mirror, or one of a different size to
the one shown here. Ask your glass
merchant to cut the mirror for you. As an
alternative to mirror, use a mirror tile. The
same technique may be used to make a
picture frame, in which case you will need
glass instead of mirror.

Using a chinagraph pencil and a ruler,
measure a 6 cm/2¼ in frame all round the
mirror. The outside of this frame is where
the pulp will be placed. Make 2 holes in
the hardboard where you wish your
picture rings to go, then push the rings
through from the smooth side and secure
them. (As this frame, with its pulp, mirror,
hardboard back and tile cement or glue, is
going to be quiet heavy, it is important
that the fixings are secure.)

Spread some undiluted glue over the
rough side of the hardboard (or use tile
cement and the ribbed spatula supplied
with it), then place the mirror on top and
press the two together firmly. Leave to dry.

2 Pat a handful of pulp (made following
instructions on p.12) on to the border
of the mirror, then take another handful
and push this against the first one. Make
sure the pulp moulds together to prevent
any cracks appearing when it dries. Repeat
this process until the whole of the frame is
covered, making sure you keep inside the

chinagraph line. If you are a messy worker, cover the inner part of the mirror with a piece of greaseproof paper to protect it.

As you work, smooth the top surface of the pulp with your hand. If you want a textured mirror frame this can be done by marking with a textured item such as a comb, or even scoring with a blunt pencil. Finally, bevel the edges slightly, as this gives a more finished appearance to the frame. Remove the protective greaseproof paper, and allow the frame to dry completely. The drying process may be accelerated by placing the frame in a warm airing cupboard where air can circulate around it.

3 When the pulp is dry, trim the outside edges with large paper scissors to ensure that they are neat and even. Cover the pulp with a layer of paper strips smeared with a 50:50 mixture of white household glue and water. The strips should come down on the inner edge to just touch the mirror; on the outer edge they should overlap on to the back of the hardboard so that everything is held in place and the edge is smooth, and the three elements of pulp, mirror and hardboard are as one and secure.

4 Clean off any gluey marks on the mirror using a glass cleaner, making sure you do not wet the paper frame.

To give a flat white surface on to which to draw and paint your design, cover the frame with 2 coats of matt white emulsion. This is an inexpensive way of priming your work. If, after 2 coats, the surface is not opaque, leave it to dry and repeat the process again. It is worth making the effort to obtain a good surface at this stage as it will affect the final finish of the mirror.

Trace off the motifs on p.II and transfer them on to the white frame. Use designer's gouache to decorate the frame, painting the motifs first and then filling in the background colour. Note how the round sun motifs fit perfectly into the corners.

Madeleine has left her bevel-edged border white on both the outer and inner edges, but you may wish instead to paint a border pattern – perhaps a gold one such as that shown on the napkin rings.

Finally, spray the frame with fixative, then brush with 2-3 coats of varnish.

Sunflower Bowl

THESE LARGE serving dishes, with their colours evocative of warmer climes,

are ideal vessels in which to serve fruit or bread at summer lunch parties.

The bowl to the right, with its stars and camels and seemingly never-ending

sand, has its inspirations in Egypt. The central bowl is decorated with

yellow and gold sunflowers in a sea of Prussian blue – the colours of Provence – and the bowl to the left, with its more controlled geometric design of large Roman numerals, is in a warm terracotta hue. One is immediately attracted by the bold size of these bowls and by their strong use of colour. The detailed designs and purity of colour seen here are characteristic of Madeleine's work.

YOU WILL NEED

MATERIALS

Newspaper strips · paper pulp · white household glue · white emulsion · designer's gouache – Prussian blue · coloured pencils · liquid gold leaf

TOOLS

Mould · petroleum jelly · bowls · pencil · large paper scissors · 2.5 cm/1 in brush · fine sandpaper · tracing paper · templates from pp.II and III · artists' paintbrushes · artists' palette · spray fixative · clear satin varnish

1 When choosing a bowl to use as a mould, make sure it does not have an inward-curving rim, as this will make it difficult – though not impossible – to release the pulped bowl from its mould. Rub a generous amount of petroleum jelly over the bowl, making sure to cover the rim as well, or cover the bowl with cling film/saran wrap (see Techniques, p.14).

Dip the strips of newspaper into a bowl of water. Squeeze off the excess water and then lay the strips on the inside of the bowl in a criss-cross fashion so that they completely cover it. Leave it to dry.

It is important not to use any diluted glue on the first layer, so that there is no possibility of the paper bowl sticking to the mould. Even with a layer of petroleum jelly applied first, there is still a slight danger of adhesion with glued strips.

2 When the strips are dry, start to lay
down a layer of pulp approximately
1 cm/½ in thick all over the newspaper.
The easiest way to do this is to start at the
bottom and work up towards the rim,
adding small pieces of pulp at a time, and
making sure they join on to the main body
of pulp. Carry on in this manner until the
inside of the bowl is completely covered in
pulped papier mâché. Allow to dry out
thoroughly in a warm room.

Pulp items do take longer to dry than
layered ones, but pulp is ideal for making
larger items such as this bowl where
stability and durability are important. (The
pulp recipe used here is the one given on
p.12, but if you want to make a heavier
bowl there are many things that can be
added to give weight and texture. These
include ground chalk or cellulose filler,
which will make the pulp feel more
substantial. Sawdust will give a textured
feel; some makers even add builder's
plaster. The more filler in a pulp, the
denser it will be; the more paste or glue,
the stronger it will be.)

3 When the pulp is completely dry,
release the pulped bowl from the
mould. If it doesn't come away easily, you
may need to break the suction between
the two; this can be done by piercing the
pulped bowl with a skewer. If for any
reason it still sticks, use a knife to lever the
two apart. Any damage done can be
mended with a layer or two of paper
strips once the bowl is free.

Draw a line round the top of the bowl
in pencil, and then use this as a guide to
trim the edge with scissors so that it is
neat and even. Cover over the top of the

bowl with a layer of strips smeared with
diluted glue. Work from the middle
outwards and make the pieces of paper
overlap at the top so that the edge of the
bowl is neat.

When this inner layer is dry, turn the
bowl over and add a layer of strips to the
underside. Again, start from the centre
and work outwards to cover all the pulp.
Leave this to dry.

4 Prime the inside of the bowl by painting it with 2 coats of white emulsion. If the surface of the bowl is still not opaque, repeat the process. When the inside is dry, turn the bowl over and do the same to the outside. Check for any roughness on the surfaces, and smooth away any bumps with sandpaper. Paint over these areas again.

Trace the sunflower design from the template on p.II and transfer it on to the bowl at repeated intervals. You can do this either by placing a sheet of carbon paper between your tracing and the bowl, and going over the design, or by scribbling over the back of your tracing, then going over the design from the front. Follow the same process for the central circles, found on p.III, or, if you wish, draw your own circles with a pair of compasses. Rub out any mistakes you make.

5 Using a combination of designer's gouache and coloured pencil, decorate the bowl, working from the centre outwards. Madeleine tends to work on one half of a bowl at a time, but you must choose the method most suitable to you and your bowl.

The patterns on this bowl comprise diamonds, triangles and stars within concentric circles, surrounded by glorious golden sunflowers. The colour palette is limited to yellow, gold, red, blue and green. Colour your design carefully, including a smart border on the inside of

the rim comprising small red and white squares. When the crayoning is complete, paint in the golden parts of the sunflowers and the golden rim with liquid gold leaf. This is a rather expensive method of gilding, but it is superior to gold gouache, which can look more yellow then gold.

If you are unsure about your painting skills, you could consider decoupage as your form of decorative medium. Carefully cut out images you like (from magazines, postcards, wrapping paper), and stick them in position with glue.

6

6 The painting of the bowl's design is completed with a background colour of deep Prussian blue. Use a fine paintbrush and take painstaking care when painting up to and between the petals of the sunflowers.

The underside of the bowl can be decorated in a similar manner – perhaps omitting the central circles and having just the sunflowers – or painted all over with the Prussian blue. Spray the bowl all over with fixative then brush on 2-3 coats of clear varnish. This will offer the bowl some protection against moisture, but it should

still not be used for moist or wet foods.

An alternative design (shown on p.36) involves the use of stylish Roman numerals in yellow and gold. The design for this bowl is reproduced on p.IV.

For the camel bowl, use the stars from the Starry Napkin Rings (template on p.II), draw your own camel template and adapt the central motif from the main project.

NATURAL CHIC

THESE TWO gleaming pitchers look fit for a Greek goddess, or perhaps Aquarius herself, to carry. These narrow-necked, fat-bellied urns echo shapes often found in Greek and Roman artefacts. The grainy, textured layers – created from oil pastels, white spirit, gold gouache and some vigorous rubbing – give an aged feel, and this technique is one which Jacqueline uses on many of her pieces, including her Twinkling Stars, Gilded Bowl and Musical Box featured in this chapter. The distressed look of these pieces is offset by the brilliantly gleaming handles, covered in gold and silver leaf.

Personalize your creations through your choice of collage items. Here Jacqueline has chosen shells, stamps, pebbles and sea-washed glass.

Twinkling Stars

THIS STARRY DECORATION is not the shiny gold that one usually associates with stars. It is, indeed, very restrained in its use of surface colour, though it makes up for this in its exuberant form of decoration. The use of oil pastels rubbed over emulsion paint gives the surface of the star a weathered-stone appearance. The swirls that make up the central decoration are made from interior filler piped from an icing bag. These are very evocative of the embroidery found in Asian cultures, whilst the centre of the star, a tiny mirror, is reminiscent of sisha mirrors that adorn the clothes of women living in India, Pakistan, Afghanistan and Tibet.

The size of the central mirror could be made much larger, if desired, with the raised decoration moved out to the points. Alternatively, the star itself could be made smaller so as to be suitable for hanging on a Christmas tree or using as part of a mobile.

A star is just one possible shape for some twinkling decorations. Shown here are four contrasting designs – all variations on the main decorative theme.
The top circle is virtually covered with large plaster swirls, and the mirror itself is surrounded by concentric circles.
The crescent shape uses a more modest repeat pattern of mirrors and swirls, whilst the triangular-edged circle shows a much larger mirror with smaller patterning.
The final shape is more closely related to the star and has collage items attached to its points.

YOU WILL NEED

MATERIALS

*Sheet of cardboard or cardboard box ·
2.5 cm/1 in square of mirror glass ·
masking tape · wallpaper paste ·
newspaper strips · 3 tablespoons of
interior wall filler · glue · white emulsion ·
oil pastel crayons – black and gold ·
gold gouache · variety of collage items,
e.g. shells, foils, stamps, small pebbles ·
clear varnish · D ring · gold twine*

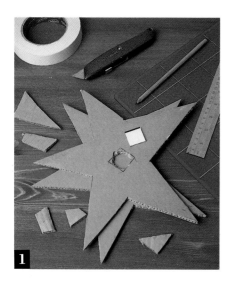

TOOLS

*Tracing paper · pencil · template on p.V ·
craft knife · cutting mat · bowl · spoon ·
small icing bag and nozzle · two 5 cm/
2 in paintbrushes · paper tissues · turps
substitute or white spirit · saucer ·
darning needle*

1 Trace the star shape from p.V on to
the cardboard and, using a craft knife,
cut out 2 stars. If you wish to make them
larger than the shape provided, enlarge
your tracing on a photocopier. Place the
2.5 cm/1 in mirror square on to one of the
card stars and draw round the mirror
square. Remove the mirror and draw a
circle within the square. Cut out the circle.
Using masking tape, secure the mirror to
the star so that it can be seen through the
aperture. Masking tape the 2 stars
together with the mirror sandwiched
between them.

2 Use small pieces of pasted newspaper
(see Techniques, p.10) to cover the
star. Apply at least 2 layers of paper, and
try to keep the paper taut as you wrap it
over the star's points. If the paper is not
stretched tightly round, your star's points
will lose their definition and crispness.
Leave to dry for at least 2 hours.

Mix the interior filler with a little water
until it is smooth and thick. (An option is
to buy ready-mixed filler, but this can
prove rather stiff to work with.) Drop the
nozzle into the icing bag, then place a
small amount of filler into the bag. Wrap

3 Scribble oil pastels on to both the back and front of the star, going over the raised design as well. Dip some tissue into the turps, and rub the colour firmly into the surface. Remove any excess colour and turps with a clean tissue.

Dip a clean tissue into some water and then squeeze out the excess. Pick up a small amount of gold gouache on the tissue and rub it vigorously on to the star until the oil colour and the gold paint split and create a broken surface.

the bag top round your finger, so that when you squeeze it you 'ice' the star rather than your wrist, then gently squeeze out your pattern around the mirror. Don't aim for perfection; and if you get any breaks in the flow because of air bubbles, just move the nozzle back a little and start again.

Leave to dry for at least an hour, then apply a layer of diluted glue over the filler to secure it to the paper surface. Leave this to dry. Paint the star with 2 coats of white emulsion, leaving ½ an hour's drying time between coats.

4 Once your surface decoration is complete, choose your collage items and stick them on with glue. Jacqueline concentrated on the centre of her star, but you could adorn your star's points instead of, or as well as, the centre. Paint all over with the varnish – excluding the mirror.

If the star is to be hung from a wall, then secure a D ring to the back of one of its points. If it is to be suspended (e.g. from a Christmas tree branch), then pierce a hole in one of the points with a large darning needle, and thread some gold twine through this.

Seashore Urn

THE SOPHISTICATION of this urn belies the fact that it is made, quite simply, from paper strips layered over a balloon. A shaped-paper neck and some cardboard handles complete the basic structure, and by this very simple method of construction a work of great charm is born.

The most striking appeal is the gleaming, distressed decoration, created using Jacqueline's technique of gold gouache over oil pastel crayons, which you can also see in evidence on her other pieces of work in this book. The handles for this strong, light piece are provided in the template section, and you will see that you can also use these handles for the Gilded Bowl and Musical Box.

Once the colouring and gilding are complete, the urn is then decorated with findings from the seashore – sand, shells and pieces of sea-washed glass wrapped in fuse wire.

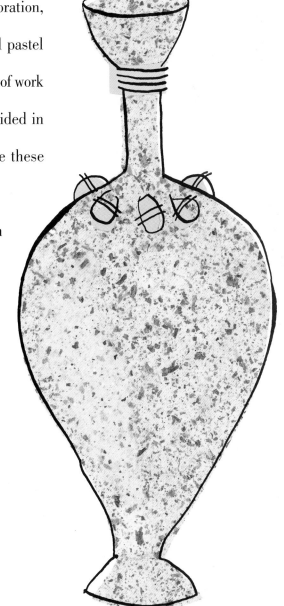

RIGHT *This more elegantly shaped vase is a variation on the Seashore Urn. The central body is still formed round a balloon, but it now sits on a shaped base, made from paper strips. The slender neck is made from a cardboard tube, taped in place, and the curved lip is formed as for the urn.*

YOU WILL NEED

MATERIALS
Newspaper strips · wallpaper paste · sheet of cardboard · masking tape · white emulsion · oil pastel crayons – black and grey · gold gouache · size · transfer gold leaf · white household glue · sand · collage items, e.g. shells, glass, etc. · aerosol clear satin varnish

TOOLS
Round balloon · string · tracing paper · pencil · template on p.VI · craft knife · cutting mat · scissors · 5 cm/2 in paintbrush · paper tissues · turps substitute or white spirit · 2.5 cm/1 in paintbrush

1 Blow up the balloon and secure the end tightly. Grasp the balloon firmly, and cover it with 3 or 4 layers of pasted newsprint strips (see Techniques, p.10), leaving a gap at the top and bottom of the balloon. (Jacqueline does this process sitting down with the balloon held between her legs, which are covered with a towel to protect her clothes.) Tie some string around the neck of the balloon and

suspend it in a warm room. Leave it to dry thoroughly, at least overnight. (It is important that the balloon does not get too cool, because it will wither and lose its shape, and so will the papier mâché surround.) When the paper is dry, pop the balloon and remove it. Trim the top and bottom with scissors so that you have 2 round holes, then, using long strips of pasted newspaper, cover the hole on the narrow end of the shape. Use 4 layers of strips. Make sure the pot will stand without wobbling. Leave it to dry for at least an hour.

Hold the pot securely and build up the neck using small strips of pasted paper. Place several strips of paper vertically on the outside edge of the pot, so they stand proud by about 5 cm/2 in. Then secure similar-length strips of paper to the inside edge of the pot. The strips will support themselves to form the neck. Use 2 layers to produce a solid neck. Then use the same technique to build the pot's lip. Bend the strips to an angle of 45 degrees to produce a shaped lip. Leave it to dry completely.

2 While the neck is drying, trace off 2 handles (one in reverse) from the template on p.VI and cut them out from card. Secure them to the urn with masking tape, then cover the handles – and the join – with small strips of pasted newspaper.

When the lip and neck are dry, trim them gently with scissors to remove the uneven lip edge.

Once the pot is completely dry, paint the entire shape with white emulsion, using the 2.5cm/1in brush. To make the paintbrush longer to reach the base and inside of the urn, attach it to a stick with masking tape. Paint the pot twice to ensure a good surface.

Cover the urn, including the inside of the lip and neck, with oil pastel. Rub the pastel in with a tissue dipped in turps, which will blend the colours together. Remove excess colour and turps with a clean tissue. Dip a new tissue in water, squeeze out the excess water, and then dip it into the gold gouache. Rub it briskly over the entire surface of the urn, until the gold paint separates.

Using the smaller brush, cover the neck and the top of the urn with size, then gently press strips of gold leaf over the surface of the pot. Use the same technique to apply gold leaf to the handles. Note that the gold leaf will not lie as a flat smooth layer but will come off in small pieces as you gently remove the backing paper.

3 Once the gold leaf is dry, dilute a little glue slightly and brush it over the top of the urn. Sprinkle a little sand over the glue, then tap the urn to remove any excess. Once the glue and sand are secure, apply handmade paper ripped into 8 pieces, 4 for the front and 4 for the back. This is best done before the sand is dry as the paper will stick better.

4 Stick your chosen collage items to the base of the neck with glue. Once these items, the sand and the paper are dry, spray the urn with varnish. If the varnish is omitted, the gold leaf will tarnish.

Gilded Bowl

IT IS HARD TO BELIEVE that this bowl started life as humble newspaper and glue strips based on a balloon. After the initial papier mâché shape was formed, the base was added, and then the handles cut from the card templates in the back of the book. For inspiration for both shape and decorative detail, this artist looks at archaeological findings, particularly

those of Saxon England. The raised swirl patterns, made from interior wall filler, on the base and rim of the bowl are reminiscent of those found on the borders of Roman togas. The oil pastel patterns are rubbed down with tissue dipped in white spirit, then given a layer of gouache to produce a distressed patination to the surface. The contrasting richness of the handles, border and interior are sheets of gold leaf. Finally, minute mementos are stuck on to the bowl's interior.

YOU WILL NEED

MATERIALS

Newspaper strips · white household glue · good-quality cartridge paper · thick cardboard · masking tape · interior wall filler · water · white emulsion · soft oil pastel crayons – black and grey · turps substitute or white spirit · gold gouache · size · gold leaf sheets · epoxy resin · collage items, e.g. shells, buttons, stamps, pieces of old lace, old letters, etc. · aerosol clear varnish

TOOLS

Balloon (measuring 37.5 cm/15 in high when inflated) · 1 cm/½ in brush · large black felt pen · scissors · pencil · template on p.VI · craft knife · large yogurt pot · icing bag and 6 mm/¼ in nozzle · 5 cm/2 in brush · toilet tissue · small bowl · plate · soft dry brush

1 Cover the round end of the balloon with 5 layers of 5 cm/2 in strips of glued newspaper (see Techniques, p.10), up to a height of about 12.5 cm/5 in. (If uncertain, draw a black line around the balloon to mark the bowl's height.) Place the bowl near a source of heat or in sunlight and leave to dry completely (for 3-4 hours near heat or overnight in a warm room). Remove the balloon.

During the drying time, make the base and the handles. Cut a strip of cartridge paper approximately 4 cm/1½ in wide and long enough for the balloon to sit on

comfortably. Join in a circle using masking tape to form the base. Trace off the handle shape from the template section (p.VI) twice on to thick card (once in reverse). Cut out the shape using a craft knife. Using small pieces of masking tape, secure the handles and base to the outside of the bowl. Cover the base and handles with pieces of glued newspaper (2.5 cm/1 in wide for the base and 6 mm/ ¼ in wide for the handles), securing them tightly to the bowl. Leave to dry for 2-3 hours in a warm, airy place.

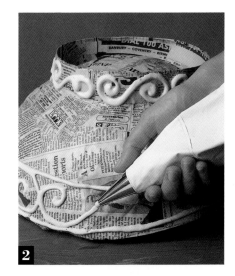

2 Mix enough interior filler (thickish but not stiff) to fill the large yogurt pot. Spoon it into the icing bag with nozzle, then 'ice' your pattern around the base and top edge, turning the bowl slowly to ensure an even flow. When it is set, brush glue well over the design with the 1cm/ ½ in brush, then paint the bowl with 2-3 coats of emulsion with the larger brush, leaving ½ an hour between coats.

3 Scribble all over the surface with oil pastel (see exterior). Wrap a few sheets of tissue round two fingers and dip into a bowl of turps substitute, then rub vigorously over the colour on the bowl. Wipe off any excess colour with dry tissue. Lightly dampen some tissue with water, then dip into some gold gouache and rub well on to the surface (see interior). Wipe bowl with clean tissue to remove any excess paint, leaving a metallic sheen.

4 You need cool hands for gold-leaf work; practise using tiny strips on some card before decorating your bowl. Cut sheets of gold leaf into strips 5 cm/ 2 in x 1 cm/½ in for the handles, 10 cm/ 4 in x 1 cm/½ in for the base and 10 cm/ 4 in x 5 cm/2 in for the interior. Brush size over all the areas to be gold-leafed, then gently press the strips of leaf on to the surfaces, and pat with a soft dry brush to adhere it to the bowl. Leave to dry for a short time then brush the surface with the soft dry brush to remove any excess leaf. Use epoxy resin to attach collage items, then lightly spray with varnish.

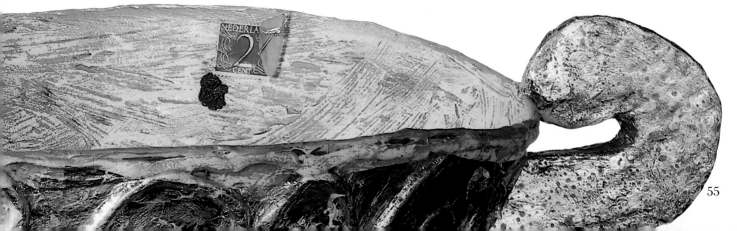

Musical Box

THERE IS SOMETHING magical about music, not only as an auditory experience but also as a visual feast. These boxes do not play music – although it would be simple enough to fit the necessary mechanism – but they do use music as a very effective form of decoration. The formal lines of the stave and the energetic dancing flow of the notes, make such wonderful rhythmic patterns that it is no surprise that music has become a very popular form of decoration for artists.

The boxes stand firmly on golden ball feet and a further golden ball is used as a lid handle for one. The arabesque handles are equally at home on the sides or the lid, and the contrast between their rounded form and the angular boxes adds a dramatic finishing flourish.

The gilded handles and feet, and the wonderful selection of collage items Jacqueline has chosen, transform simple boxes into glorious ones.

RIGHT *The construction of these boxes is simplicity itself: sections of card taped and glued together. To form the domed lid of the box shown far right you will need to find a cup or bowl that fits on top of your box, and layer your papier mâché over this.*

YOU WILL NEED

MATERIALS

Large sheet of cardboard or strong box · masking tape · white household glue · wallpaper paste · newspaper strips · balsa wood block 15 x 15 x 15 cm/6 x 6 x 6 in · white emulsion · oil pastel crayons – black and grey · gold gouache · size · 4 sheets transfer gold leaf · assortment of collage pieces · aerosol clear satin varnish

TOOLS

Pencil · ruler · cutting mat · craft knife · scissors · 1 cm/½ in brush · tracing paper · handle template from p. VI · small hacksaw · sandpaper · 1.5 cm/1 in brush · paper tissues · turps substitute or white spirit · saucer · soft brush

1 Draw 4 equal squares on to the cardboard, each measuring 12.5 x 12.5 cm/5 x 5 in. Using a sharp craft knife, cut them out and join them together along their sides with lengths of masking tape to form a box shape. Do your cutting on a cutting mat or, failing that, a wadge of newspaper. Measure the internal size of the base of the box and cut a piece of card to this size. Push the card into the base of the box and secure it there with masking tape to form the bottom.

To make the lid, measure the external dimensions of the top of the box and cut

2 pieces of card to fit exactly on top of the box. Then cut 2 smaller pieces of card (slightly smaller than the internal measurements of the top of the box); these will become the base of the lid. Glue the 2 smaller pieces of card on to the 2 larger ones (as shown) and leave to dry.

While the lid is drying, trace off the handle template from p.VI and cut out 2 handles from the remaining cardboard (one of which must be reversed). Secure these card handles to the sides of the box with masking tape, making sure they are firm and at the same height.

2 Cover the entire box, including the lid and handle, with at least 3 layers of small strips of newspaper coated with wallpaper paste (see Techniques, p.10). Leave the box to dry in a warm room for 4-6 hours.

Use the 2.5 cm/1 in brush to paint the entire box and lid, inside and out, with 2 coats of white emulsion, leaving ½ an hour's drying time between the coats. Leave to dry completely.

Using the hacksaw, cut a 2.5 cm/1 in slice from the balsa wood. Then cut this slice into 9 equal blocks (dividing the slice up as though for a game of noughts and crosses). Discard 4. Use the craft knife to shave the corners and edges off the remaining 5 small blocks of balsa, being careful always to work away from your hand to avoid any danger of cutting yourself. Smooth the blocks into approximate spheres with the sandpaper. Turn the box upside down and attach 4 of the balls to the base with glue and the remaining ball to the centre of the lid. Leave to dry for at least an hour. Paint the balls white.

3 Scribble over the outside of the box and lid with oil pastels. Dip pieces of tissue into the turps and rub the colour into the box surface. Remove any excess colour and turps with clean tissues. Then, using the 2.5 cm/1 in brush, pick up some colour from the box and rub it on to the feet and handle. Dry with a clean tissue.

Dip a clean tissue into some water and squeeze out any excess, then pick up a small amount of gold gouache and rub it over the surface of the box and lid. Repaint the interior of the box if it has become stained in the colouring process.

4 Cut 4 sheets of gold leaf into approximately 2.5 cm/1 in squares. Holding the box firmly, and using the 1 cm/½ in brush, cover the first ball foot with size, then pick up individual pieces of leaf and press them gently on to the foot. Remove the backing paper, and rub over with the soft dry brush. Repeat for the other 3 feet and the ball handle. Leave them to dry before using the same technique to cover the card handles.

When the gold leaf is dry, use a selection of collage items to decorate your box, then spray it with clear satin varnish.

PASTEL ELEGANCE

MELANIE WILLIAMS' home in rural Wales has been the inspiration for much of her work. The flora and fauna around Bronllys castle – its name a reminder of a bygone era – have been carefully observed and then re-created in delicately shaded papier mâché. Subtlety is achieved by layering colours one upon another and then gently rubbing the surface with sandpaper to reveal some of the hidden colours beneath. The slightly warm, sun-bleached look that results is as much a tribute to Melanie's idyllic pastoral home as it is to her love of the faded tones of Victoriana.

A pastel clock, a floral cup and some delicate tulips all seem to glow with the same translucent light.

Farmyard Mobile

MAGICAL MOBILES moving in the breeze give pleasure to both adults and children. A mobile is often the very first 'toy' given to a baby, the combination of movement and colour being something on which to focus. The naive simplified shapes of these rounded farm animals are deliberately out of scale so that they balance one another in equilibrium. They are similar to many animals found in children's nursery books, but unlike illustrations they are three-dimensional and subtle in tone and texture. These colourings are very delicate and deliberately uneven, and the animals have a 'weather-beaten' charm of their own.

Full details are given for suspending your animals as a mobile. An alternative use for them could be to turn them into fridge magnets to accompany Madeleine's Stripy Fish Magnets (see p.24).

Paper, glue, cotton and kebab sticks are transformed by skill and paint into this charming mobile.

YOU WILL NEED

MATERIALS

Mount card · newspaper strips · flour and water paste · white emulsion · poster colours · matt or gloss polyurethane varnish · 1 x 19 cm/7½ in wooden kebab stick · 2 x 16 cm/6½ in wooden kebab sticks · paperclips · white household glue · coloured embroidery thread

TOOLS

Tracing paper · pencil · templates on pp.VII and VIII · scalpel · cutting mat · bowl · fine grade sandpaper · 1 cm/½ in paintbrush · paper tissues · palette · artists' paintbrush · very fine paintbrush · wire cutters · needle · scissors

1 Trace the animal templates from pp.VII and VIII and transfer them on to thick card. Cut out the shapes using a scalpel and resting on either a cutting mat or some newspapers. Smear some flour and water paste on to the newspaper strips, and cover the animals with 2-3 layers of these on both sides. Where the strips stick out beyond the animal shapes, bend them round firmly to the other side, making sure you keep the paper quite taut. Tails and beaks, etc. will require careful work to ensure they remain identifiable.

2 Once the animal shapes are fully dry, proceed to smooth them down with the fine grade sandpaper, then cover them with a layer of white emulsion to prime the surface. Smooth down once more with sandpaper. Now use the artists' brush and some poster paints to give the animals their base colours, dabbing the paint off with tissues for an uneven effect. (If you prefer, use gouache or watercolours.)

3 Apply more detail to each of the animals. Use sandpaper to create a textured effect by applying paint then partly rubbing it away while it is still wet. Using the very fine paintbrush, apply dapple to the horse, feathers to the cockerel, and other fur and feather details to the other animals and birds. Once they are completely dry, apply a coat of polyurethane varnish.

4 Paint the kebab sticks (or use thin dowelling) in bright colours. Use the longest length at the top of the mobile and the smaller ones below (see diagram showing how to hang your mobile). Snip the top off some paperclips to create small loops from which to hang the animals. Using a needle, make holes at the centre of the top of the animals and birds, though in the case of the duck the holes should go slightly towards the head to enable the bird to balance correctly. Place a blob of glue on the ends of the loops and insert them into the holes on the animals' and birds' backs. Leave them to dry.

Cut lengths of coloured embroidery thread to contrast with the animals. Attach one end of each piece to the kebab sticks and the other end to an animal or bird. Move the pieces of thread along the sticks until the mobile balances.

Daisy, Daisy

THE VERY ESSENCE of daisies has been captured in these papier mâché flowers, made by layering small strips of paper over shaped lengths of wire. Note the gradation of colour, very similar to that of real daisies. By a judicious spattering of colour on to the petals a texture is achieved which helps to break up the surface colour on the daisies and to create more authentic looking petals.

Once the principles of construction have been understood, you can vary the technique to create all kinds of flowers in many different sizes. Pick flowers and leaves and carefully observe just how they are constructed in order to help you make your own flowers. The joy of using wire to form the petals is that it bends, so the basic outline can be constructed before the paper strips are applied.

Pansies and tulips are but two examples of other flowers you could make with papier mâché. The graceful stalks and drooping leaves of the tulip are easy to form with wire. When attaching petals to the flower middle, for any kind of flower, vary the number of petals for a natural effect.

YOU WILL NEED

MATERIALS
Wire in fine and thin thicknesses · flour and water paste · thin strips of newspaper · white household glue · white emulsion · poster paints – off-white, pink, yellow and green · varnish (matt or gloss)

TOOLS
Wire cutters · templates on p.IX · bowl · fine sandpaper · needle · artists' brushes · palette

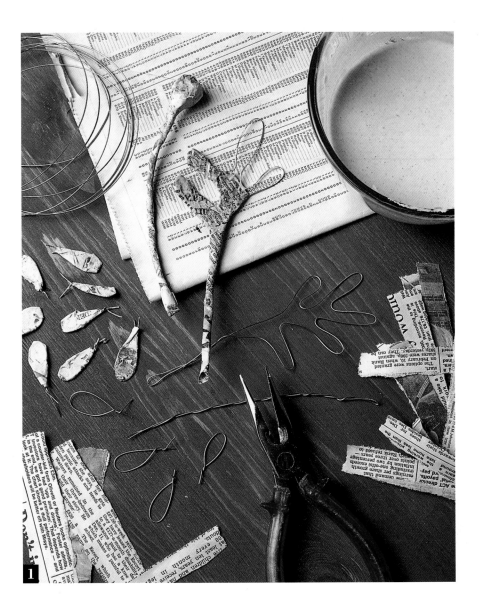

1 Bend the fine wire into daisy petal shapes by simply looping the wire and then wrapping one end round the other. You will need to make between 36 and 40 petals, allowing 5 to 6 for each flower.

Make leaf shapes following the outlines provided on p.IX. Using these outlines will enable you to make petals and leaves of suitable sizes. At the base of the leaf shape twist the wire together to form a stem. Cut the thin wire into lengths for the flower stems, bend each length in half, then twist the two halves loosely together.

Smear some paper strips with flour and water paste. Mould the pasted paper into balls to make flower middles, and stick them on the tops of the stems. Finally, wrap 2-3 layers of pasted paper strips around the petals, leaves and flower stems. Leave to dry.

2 When all the flower parts are fully dry, sand them down until they are smooth. Make holes round the outside of the flower middles using a needle.

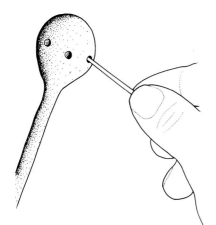

Cut off one of the two pieces of wire forming the petals so that only one piece stands proud. Place a blob of glue into each hole and then insert the petals one by one. Don't aim to create perfectly regular flowers. Some irregularity adds to their charm. Leave to dry.

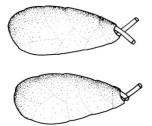

3 Paint the flowers, leaves and stems with a coat of white emulsion to act as a base coat for the decoration.

To give the daisies an authentic look, it is best to spatter your chosen colours gently over the white, leaving a delicate, natural appearance. Use off-white, pink and green on the petals, varying your use to give each flower some individuality, and spatter them by holding the head of the brush back with your finger then quickly releasing it. Paint the flower middles yellow and the remainder of each stem green.

When all the paint is dry, give the flowers and leaves a coat of varnish.

Another favourite flower of Melanie's is the tulip, and these can look very realistic in papier mâché (see p.61). The long, flat leaves and the slightly square petals require no extra skills; just remember to bend the wire form of the leaves (before covering them in paper) to varying degrees for a naturalistic look.

Country Jug

RIGHT *These jugs make a very pretty display on this rustic shelf. If you want to use your jug to hold flowers, insert a small jam jar of water inside the jug.*
BELOW *To accompany your jug, try your hand at a matching or contrasting cup. You won't be able to drink out of it, but it will look charming.*

THESE JUGS look good enough for serving cream at a country tea party. Decorate them with spots, flowers or a mosaic pattern – with or without an inset scene – or invent your own design. The choice is endless and the results charming.

The wonder of papier mâché is that you can construct almost anything from it. These pretty looking jugs were formed round china jugs, avoiding the handles. After three layers had been applied and had dried, the papier mâché case was cut away from the original and then joined together with strips to form a new jug. This method of cutting and rejoining a papier mâché shape means that you can choose existing moulds of some complexity around which to layer your paper.

YOU WILL NEED

MATERIALS

*Newspaper strips · flour and water
paste · wire · white emulsion · poster
paints · matt or gloss varnish*

TOOLS

*Jug for mould · petroleum jelly · bowl ·
scalpel · knife · finegrade sandpaper ·
2.5 cm/1 in paintbrush · artists' brushes*

1 Cover the jug with a thin layer of
petroleum jelly, making sure no areas
are missed. Avoid the handle completely
throughout this stage, as it will be made
separately in stage 2. First cover the jug in
a layer of plain newspaper strips (without
any glue). This will prevent the paper
sticking to any areas of the mould that
were not sufficiently covered with jelly.
Then apply 2 layers of strips smeared with
the flour and water paste to the mould
(see Techniques, p.10). Press the papier
mâché down well to avoid getting air
bubbles. Leave to dry overnight.

When the papier mâché jug is fully dry,
use a scalpel to cut a line down the jug
where the handle is situated and another
one directly opposite it (i.e. under the
spout). Take this cut round under the base
of the papier mâché jug until it meets the
first cut. Now prise the papier mâché away
from the mould. It should come off easily,
but if it is reluctant, slip a knife inside the
edge to ease it off.

2 Place the 2 halves of the paper jug back together again and cover the entire jug with 2 or 3 layers of strips.

To make the handle, cut a piece of wire, about double the length of the existing handle, fold it in half and twist the halves together, then bend it into a handle shape. Pierce the handle through the jug and bend the wire inside the jug to stop it coming back out. Use 2-3 layers of paste and paper strips round the handle to form its shape and to secure it to the jug at the top and bottom. Neaten the rim of the jug with more strips of paper and leave it to dry. When it is fully dry, smooth down the jug with the sandpaper to a wood-like finish, then prime it with white emulsion.

3 This jug is decorated using a very simple but highly effective technique of layering and rubbing back to create a distressed appearance. Paint over your white emulsion with a coat of bright pink poster paint. Once this is dry, apply another coat of white emulsion. For your final coat, apply some mid-blue poster paint. Leave the jug until the paint is dry, then rub with the sandpaper to reveal the colours beneath. Vary your pressure so that you rub back to different layers over the jug's surface, but be careful not to rub so hard that you go back to the paper itself.

4 Paint the handle and the inside of the jug with the bright pink. When this is dry, carefully paint a polka dot pattern in dark blue on the jug. When the dots are dry, coat with a clear varnish.

73

ANNE OF WINDY WILLOWS   L.M. Montgomery

POEMS FOR 9-YEAR-OLDS AND UNDER   CHOSEN BY KIT WRIGHT

SCOTTISH FOLK AND FAIRY TALES   Ed. Gordon Jarvie

ROALD DAHL   Charlie and the Chocolate Factory

LITTLE LORD FAUNTLEROY   FRANCES HODGSON BURNETT

The Turbulent Term of Tyke Tiler   GENE KEMP

Stig of the Dump   CLIVE KING

STORIES FOR NINE-YEAR-OLDS   edited by Sara and Stephen Corrin

OLIVER, AMANDA AND GRANDMOTHER PIG   JEAN VAN LEEUWEN

KING TUBBITUM AND THE HAIRY MAMMOTH   MARGARET RYAN

WILLIAM AND THE WOLVES   DEREK SAMPSON

ENGLISH FAIRY TALES   JOSEPH JACOBS

The Sky-moos

The Hoopicopter

Shepherd's Clock

THE PASTEL GREEN grass and staring sheep make this clock an eye-catching feature. Many people would hesitate at the idea of making something as complex as a clock, and yet with the advent of quartz movements, which can be purchased for very little money and fitted easily, it is an exciting object to make.

This clock is built on a cardboard base, and the stepped sides give it an art deco air, but if you wanted a simpler shape you could use a cardboard box. The clock face can be purchased or hand-painted, and if you do not trust yourself to paint the numerals, leave them blank. In this way your clock can be as simple as you wish.

The grass green colouring of the clock, with its delicate border decoration, makes a gentle background for the slightly 'muddied' wool of the sheep and the distressed pale mauve of the clock face.

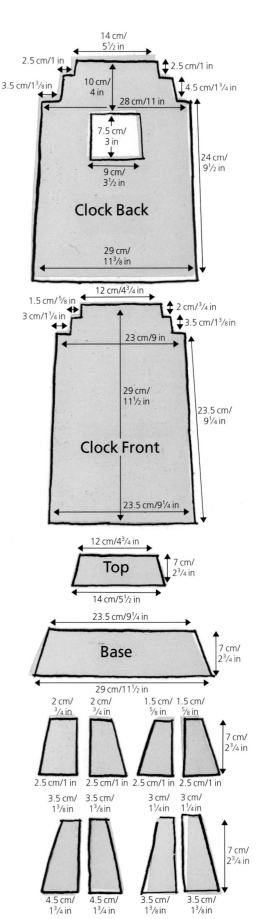

This delicate, yet striking, clock would make a delightful addition to any child's room. The fine-painted border detail emphasizes the unusual shape of the clock. To construct the basic clock shape, draw all the pattern pieces shown here on the mount card, cut them out with a craft knife then tape them together.

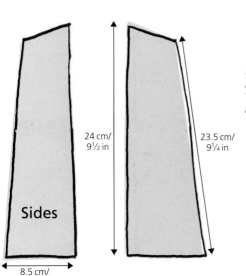

YOU WILL NEED

MATERIALS

A2 sheet of mount card · masking tape · flour and water paste · newspaper strips · white emulsion · poster colours – grass green, white, brown, pale mauve, red and blue · clock mechanism, hands and battery · matt or gloss varnish

TOOLS

Pencil · metal ruler · craft knife · cutting mat · bowl · pen · fine sandpaper · artists' palette · 1 cm/^{1}/$_2$ in brush · artists' brushes · bradawl

1 Using the measurements provided on p.75, draw the pattern pieces for the clock on to your mount card, including a 12.5 cm/5 in diameter circle for the clock face. Then, using a craft knife with a metal ruler or straight edge to guide you, and working on a cutting mat, cut out the shapes. Build the basic clock shape by sticking the pieces together with masking tape. Use the measurements on the diagram to place the 8 wedge-shaped pieces that form the 'steps' at the top.

Once the body of the clock is complete, tape 2 small oblongs of 3 layers of card

each to the back of the clock face so that it will stand proud from the clock body.

2 Tape the clock face in position. Smear some flour and water paste on to your strips of newspaper, and use these to cover the cardboard clock body and face. As you work, make sure that some of the strips overlap from the front and back on to the top and sides, as this will strengthen the construction and help to make the clock rigid. When covering the join between the clock face and the front of the clock, make sure that the outline is left

crisp. This is done by taking care to push each piece of paper down firmly around the edge of the circle. Cover everything with 3-4 layers and leave to dry.

Using the template on p.X, mark the position of the sheep on the clock front with a pen. Scrunch up a piece of newspaper into a ball and dip it into the paste. Gently, but firmly, push it on to the clock face in a place where a sheep's position is marked. Repeat this process for the other sheep. Leave them to dry, laying the clock down on its back.

3 Cover the sheep's bodies with strips of paper and paste to give them a smoother surface and also to help to anchor them to the clock front. Also cover the rest of the clock and its face with a further layer of strips. Leave to dry.

Smooth down the whole surface with fine sandpaper and coat it with a layer of white emulsion. Sand again, and paint once more if necessary.

4 Mix grass green paint with a little white and apply with a large artists' brush, avoiding the clock face.

Mix some white with a tiny amount of brown to create a dirty off-white sheep's wool colour. Use this to colour the sheep. Leave the paint to dry. To give the sheep a textured coat, rub gently with sandpaper. Using a finer brush, paint in the sheep's legs and faces with black paint.

Paint the background of the clock face pale mauve and rub it gently with sandpaper to reveal some of the white paint below the surface. To add definition to the clock body, paint a border pattern of red squiggles and blue dots with a fine brush.

5 Push a bradawl into the centre of the clock face to create a hole for fitting the clock mechanism. Enlarge the hole with a pencil or the handle of a paintbrush to the right size for the mechanism screw.

Draw the clock numerals on by hand, using pencil so that you can rub out any mistakes. Paint the numerals in black.

Finally, fit the clock mechanism to the back of the clock, with the hands on the front, and insert the battery. If you wish, the clock may be varnished for extra protection, but you must remove the clock hands first.

COLLAGE
CREATIONS

LIKE MOST OF US, Gerry Copp started making papier mâché as a child. In adult life it was her concern with the environment that brought her back to it. By experimenting, she found that she could make highly decorative objects by collaging sheets of handmade recycled paper on to papier mâché forms. One of the advantages of the way in which she works is that she requires no paints or dyes to provide a decorative finish. Her work is a continual exploration of new materials, including sweet wrappers and foil papers. The results are highly imaginative and colourful pieces of work.

Coloured papers are the only form of decoration that Gerry uses and yet the results are still varied and highly appealing.

Brilliant Brooch

FOR A PIECE OF jewellery to be beautiful it does not have to be made from intrinsically valuable materials. It is the composition, the way in which the chosen materials are used together and the textures all work in unison, that helps to create something special. If you analyse the jewellery shown here you will see that it comprises simply card, torn paper and a very small amount of gold leaf. Yet the colours are very carefully chosen so that they work well together, and the fine line drawn round the different elements of the design helps to pull those elements together.

YOU WILL NEED

MATERIALS
Card · white paper strips · white household glue · handmade or recycled papers · coloured cartridge paper – pale and dark blue · transfer gold leaf · brooch finding · two-part epoxy resin

TOOLS
Tracing paper · pencil · template on p.XI · scissors · craft knife or scalpel · fine line ink pen · artists' paintbrush · soft dry brush

1 Jewellery is often a great introduction to the craft of papier mâché because it is small scale and thus quite quick to produce. To make this brooch, trace the template from p.XI and transfer the shape on to card. Cut out the shape with scissors. Smear some glue on to the strips of white paper, then cover both sides of the card shape with 3 layers of the strips. Leave to dry for about 2 days.

If you want to make a pair of matching earrings, scale down the template and cut 2 shapes from card. Follow the instructions as for making the brooch.

2 To cover the brooch, choose either some handmade or recycled paper: anything with an added fibre or parts of plants will add interest to the final piece. Stick the paper on with glue then leave it to dry before completing the design.

Using a fine line ink pen, draw a border line close to the edge of the brooch. This line helps to define the shape of the brooch. Draw a star shape on to pale blue cartridge paper, then cut it out with a scalpel or craft knife. Draw a fine blue line close to the edge of the star.

Tear circles of different sizes from both light and dark blue cartridge paper. Tearing the paper rather than cutting it makes for a more pleasing natural shape. If you do not find tearing circles easy then draw the circles on the back of the paper by tracing round (for example) a coin. Tear very gently round the outside of the drawn circles.

Although the project here uses different shades of blue as a colourway, you can use different colours and combinations of colours to complement the outfit with which the brooch will be worn. The joy of decorating with paper is that you can experiment by placing the pieces on their background and trying new combinations until you are satisfied.

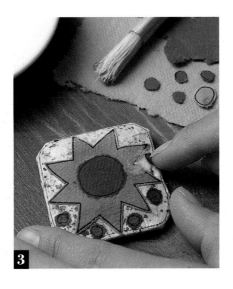

3 Once you are sure of the colour combinations you like, then brush glue on to one side of the large circle and stick it on to the centre of the star shape. Stick the smaller circles between the points of the stars.

If you wish to go into jewellery production (and there is no doubt that these items will make very welcome presents) then construct and decorate a few pieces at a time. In this way you can try different shapes of brooches and earrings and also make small pieces for necklaces and bracelets.

4 Add concentric circles to the middle circle in different colours. Add fine lines round the edge of these. Brush glue on to the brooch and then, while it is still tacky, rub on the transfer gold leaf randomly to add a sparkle to the brooch. This is done by cutting the leaf into thin strips and then gently placing them on the brooch and pulling off the backing paper and then rubbing with the soft dry brush.

Stick the brooch finding on to the back of the brooch using two-part epoxy resin. Follow the maker's instructions for the resin's drying time.

Mosaic Plate

This gleaming plate, created from pulped papier mâché formed over a mould, is decorated with small pieces of cartridge and foil papers to resemble mosaic.

THIS PLATE IS NOT mosaic made from glass or ceramic tiles, but it is a pulped papier mâché plate decorated with foil tesserae, the building blocks that form mosaics. In real mosaics the tesserae are laid in sequential order, and this is so in the case of this bowl, where the rim has a precisely laid triangular pattern and the inner layer of turquoise appears to be more random. Note how the scale of the piece changes towards the centre of the neat rows; this helps to draw attention towards the centre of the plate and the centre of the star. The colours used on this mosaic evoke those found in many Mexican and other South American countries: the gleaming gold of the sun and the beautiful turquoise of the semi-precious stone from which it gets its name.

In the same way that mosaic is often made from broken bits and pieces of china and mirror, so paper mosaic requires only odds and ends of various papers, rather than pristine sheets. Keep scraps of papers, such as the brightly coloured foil wrappers of many chocolates and Easter eggs, and recycle them to decorate a mosaic plate. If you can expand this treasure-troving to all forms of paper, you will have a ready supply of material to pulp and to use for decoration, whenever the creative urge takes you.

YOU WILL NEED

MATERIALS
Paper pulp · white household glue · cartridge papers – light, mid and dark blue · foil papers – gold, silver, blues and turquoises

TOOLS
Bowl · plate · cling film/saran wrap · dress-making shears · pencil · tracing paper · scissors · artists' paintbrushes · cocktail sticks · pair of compasses or jam jar lid · ruler

1 Make the pulp according to the instructions on p.12. Cover the plate in cling film/wrap and spread the pulp evenly over it with your fingers to a depth of about 1 cm/½ in. Leave it to dry for 4 days. As long as you are not using a metal plate as the mould, and as long as you keep a careful eye on it, you can speed up the process by drying it out in a microwave oven. The best way to do this is to put it in the oven and turn it on for 10 minutes at a time. Always be there to check it does not catch fire. When it is dry, remove it from the mould and peel off the cling film/ wrap.

Use a large pair of dress-making shears to trim the edge of the bowl so that it is smooth and even.

2 Draw a regular 5-pointed star, or trace the one reproduced on p. 82, on a piece of light blue cartridge paper. Cut out the star shape with scissors. Rip some pieces of dark and mid-blue paper and brush them with a dilute 50:50 water and glue mix. Using the photograph as your guide, stick dark blue pieces round the rim of the plate. Make sure some pieces are stuck so that they overlap the

edge of the plate and fold over to the back of the rim, thus giving a neat edge.

Stick some mid-blue paper strips on to the central area of the bowl, overlapping them slightly. Do not leave any gaps between the pieces of paper and make sure they are lying flat, with no air bubbles trapped. Leave to dry and check again that you have a smooth surface and that no corners or edges of paper are uneven or unstuck. If they are, push some glue on the end of a cocktail stick or cotton bud under the offending pieces of paper, and press down firmly.

Paste the underside of the paper star, position it so that it is in the centre of the plate, and then brush more diluted glue over the top of the star. Using either a pair of compasses or the lid of a jam jar, draw a circle on some of the dark blue cartridge paper. Cut out the circle with scissors, carefully position it so that it is central, then stick this on to the middle of the star and thus the middle of the plate.

3 Mark some even-sized triangles on the gold foil paper, using a ruler and a blunt pencil to indent the back of the foil. (Foil paper can be found wrapped around some chocolates and sweets, or you can buy transfer gold leaf – often known as Dutch metal or schlag – which comes in very thin sheets.) Cut out the triangle shapes, brush them with diluted glue and stick these round the rim of the plate. Stick them next to each other, alternating the points and the bases of the triangles to achieve a neat patterned edge. As an alternative to gold foil use silver kitchen foil, or perhaps alternate the two.

4 Cut tiny foil squares in metallic blues, turquoises and silvers. (It is worth keeping foil papers from Easter eggs and Christmas tree chocolate decorations for such work as they come in interesting colours. Get rid of creases by rubbing over the surface with your forefinger, then store the papers somewhere flat.)

As tiny pieces of foil can be difficult to handle, use a cocktail stick to position them, and use undiluted glue. Work in a room free from draughts or you will find the tiny pieces have blown away.

When all the glued foils are dry, and the front of the plate is complete, turn it over and decorate the underside in the same way; or, if you prefer, make a different pattern using foils or non-metallic papers. When all the decoration is dry, brush over it with diluted glue, which will act as a varnish. If you desire a very smooth, almost lacquer-like surface, then paint it with 3 or 4 coats of undiluted glue, leaving it to dry between coats.

Although this platter is varnished and therefore partially protected, it is still not suitable for serving moist or wet food. Keep it for purely decorative purposes.

Star-rimmed Bowl

IT IS BELIEVED that cave people first translated the twinkling image of a star in the sky into its current multi-pointed shape, and it has been used as decoration in this form ever since. Gerry's bowl uses the shape of the star for its rim and the colour of the star for much of its decoration, and the completed piece is as striking in its colour as it is in its shape.

The bowl itself is made of pulp on to which the cardboard star rim fits neatly. The pattern is cleverly made up from torn paper and applied in a manner guaranteed to confuse the viewer as to whether he or she is looking at a concave or convex shape. The final yellow band provides a neat edging and emphasizes the star shape.

Shown here on some colourful mats, a collection of these bowls using different colours and designs makes a riotous display. Note how the lack of a border on the bottom bowl makes the star points look fatter.

LEFT *Roughly torn circles, triangles, squares and spirals are all you need to decorate these bowls. No paints or crayons are required. This simple form of decoration means that the exterior of each bowl is composed of the same elements as the interior: paper and glue. What could be simpler?*

YOU WILL NEED

MATERIALS

Paper pulp · cardboard · typing paper or newspaper strips · wallpaper paste · coloured cartridge papers – dark blue, yellow, green, mid-blue, pink · white household glue

TOOLS

Mould · cling film/saran wrap · bowls · craft knife or scissors · tracing paper · pencil · template from p.XII · fine sandpaper · artists' paintbrush

1 Cover your mould with some cling film/saran wrap, and then with a layer of pulp (see Techniques, p.12). When the bowl is dry, remove it from its mould. If it does not come out easily, cut it and then mend the cut with pulp. Trim the edge using a pair of scissors.

Trace off the half-rim from p.XII, then turn your tracing paper right round and trace the half-rim again, to complete the circle. Transfer this star shape on to card, then invert your papier mâché bowl in the centre of the star, and trace round it. Cut out the star-shaped rim from the card.

2 Insert the bowl into the rim. You may need to trim the bowl or rim with a craft knife or scissors to get a good fit. Fill any gaps between the rim and the bowl with pulp, taking a small amount of pulp between thumb and forefinger and gently pressing it into position. Make sure the line of pulp is continuous. When you have completed the circle of pulp, smooth it out with your finger so that there is no visible line between rim and bowl.

Once the pulp is completely dry it can be given a rub down with sandpaper to make it almost mirror-smooth.

3 Dip strips of paper into some wallpaper paste, then take off the excess by running the strips between your thumb and forefinger. It is better to use small strips of paper when working on a curved surface because they tend to lie flatter, with less danger of trapping air, and are easier to apply.

Use the strips to cover the join between the bowl and the rim and also to cover the rim itself. Layer each piece so that it slightly overlaps the piece next to it. Use 3 or 4 layers altogether. Pull the paper taut as you cover the points of the stars to

make sure that they are neatly finished.

Any bagginess, or air bubbles, here will spoil the look of the piece, so spend time laying the strips and folding them over to the rear.

4 To decorate the bowl, first tear strips of cartridge paper into different lengths and widths (see 'Torn paper', p.20). Again, do not make them too big. Apply one layer of coloured cartridge paper to the interior of the bowl and to the rim. Leave it to dry, then turn the bowl over and decorate the underside of the bowl and rim in the same manner.

Tear other coloured papers into strips, rings and dots with which to make your collaged decoration. Layer the strips to make stripes leading down into the centre of the bowl. This simple design has a clever effect of looking at once concave and convex. Place circles of varying sizes in the centre of the bowl. Paste all these with undiluted glue, and press them down with the glue brush to adhere them in place.

5 Place double circles on each star point to decorate the rim. Then add the finishing touch of some bright yellow edging which both neatens the edge and provides a sharp, eye-catching finish.

Exotic Bird

IS THIS A BIRD of paradise? It is certainly a very exotic bird cleverly constructed from chicken wire and various papers. This is a fine example of how papier mâché can be used to create quite unusual forms; the chicken wire can be shaped and moulded to any form you want, and your structures can be as big or as small as you wish. A covering of stretched tissue paper and then a layer of paper pulp builds up the body shape, including the wings and crest, and a final layer of torn paper creates a decorative finish.

By the addition of embellishments such as wire curls on the tail and crest, moulded wings, beaks and feathers a simple shape can be transformed. Use beautiful bright colours for the torn-paper plumage, and use your imagination for the embellishments. Be as bold as you want, mixing colours you might not normally put together, for a stunning result. Your bird will dazzle.

ABOVE *This fish mobile is another example of the usefulness of chicken wire: you can give your chosen shape a level of definition impossible to achieve with, for example, a balloon. Mould the fish's body, fins and tail from the wire, before covering and decorating them in the same way as for the bird.*

YOU WILL NEED

MATERIALS

Chicken wire · fuse wire · white household glue · sheets of tissue paper · paper pulp · thin card · epoxy resin · thin enamelled wire · cartridge paper – dark red, green, navy, yellow, pale blue, mid-blue and fuchsia pink

TOOLS

Protective gloves · tin snips · shallow tray · bowl · round-nosed (jewellers') pliers · artists' paintbrush

1 Wearing protective gloves, cut and roll the chicken wire into a bird shape. It is important to get the basic shape correct as it is then very easy to apply the pulped paper and to make a realistic looking bird. The best tool for cutting wire is a pair of tin snips. Chicken wire comes in different gauges; choose one with a small hole as it will be easier to work with. Unless you are used to working with wire, it can seem daunting; but do persevere – it is worth it. The important thing is to make sure that no sharp ends are sticking out as they will just poke through any papier

mâché you apply. One way of preventing the wire shape from unrolling – should it seem liable to do this – is to tie it together with a fine wire such as fuse wire.

2 Mix some glue 50:50 with water and put it in a shallow tray. Tear the tissue paper into pieces of a size that is easy to handle, and dip them into the diluted glue. Apply the first sheet of tissue to the armature (the name given to the metal body you have just made), lifting the paper up – stretching it as you do so – and pushing it on to the framework. Apply the

next piece in the same manner, making sure that there is a slight overlap where the pieces join. Leave it to dry for 2 days or until the tissue is dry.

When the tissue paper layer dries it stretches to form a drum-tight skin. This creates the surface on which to place the pulped paper.

3 Mix up the pulp according to the instructions on p.12. Pick up small pieces at a time and press them on to the tissue-covered armature. Keep applying the pulp until you have covered the frame in an even coat, about 1 cm/½ in deep.

Once the main body is covered, you can start to work on the bird's features, such as its wings, crest and tail. Build these up by squeezing small amounts of pulp between your thumb and forefinger and pressing them on to the body. If you find this does not work and that pieces are falling off, it may be that the pulp is too wet. In this case put it in a sieve and squeeze out the excess moisture before trying again.

If you have no success in sculpting the pulp in this way, there is an alternative method you can try. Leave the body of the bird to dry, and make the features such as the wings and crest separately by cutting the relevant shapes from card and applying pulp to them. Leave the shapes to dry and then stick them on to the body of the bird using a strong glue such as an epoxy resin.

4 Now comes the opportunity to let your imagination run wild as you decorate your wonderful bird. The following instructions will enable you to create a bird similar to Gerry's, but you can of course decorate your own bird in whatever way you like.

Cut a length of wire into 3 pieces of about 20 cm/8 in, and 3 pieces of about

4

10 cm/4 in. Working on one piece of wire at a time, grasp the end of it between the grips of some round-nosed pliers and curl it. When you are happy with the shape, stick the less-curled end into the bird's head or tail and anchor it in position with some pulped paper. Repeat for the other lengths of wire. Leave to dry.

Decorate the bird by ripping pieces of coloured cartridge paper into both strips and circles. Dip the pieces of dark red ripped paper into the diluted glue and apply them to the body of the bird. Next cover the wing, tail and crest with green paper. For each eye use a navy circle, a slightly smaller yellow circle and an inner pale blue circle, and for the body use circles of purple with centres of mid-blue. The final decorative flourish is a bright yellow beak and fuchsia pink dots on the bright green wings.

To protect the bird, paint it with a coat of diluted or undiluted glue. This looks white when it is applied but will dry clear. Alternatively, there are some very good quick-drying acrylic varnishes available that are suitable for items such as this.

Suppliers

Because the raw materials for papier mâché are so basic and the tools and materials needed are mostly household ones, there is little need for the papier mâché maker to visit specialist art supply shops. Anything you might have difficulty in finding can be found at the shops listed below. *Mail order available.

UK

London Graphic Centre
Unit 9-10 McKay Trading Estate
Kensal Road, London W10 5BN
0181 969 6644 (and branches)

E. Plotons*
273 Archway Road
London
0181 348 0315
(for metal leaf)

Falkiner Fine Paper*
76 Southampton Row
London WC1B 4AR
0171 831 1151

T.N. Lawrence & Son
119 Clerkenwell Road
London EC1R 5BY
0171 242 3534

Paper Chase*
213 Tottenham Court Road
London W1P 9AF
0171 580 8496 (and branches)

US

Sam Flax
111 8th Avenue
New York NY 10011
212 620 3060

Sax Arts and Crafts
PO Box 51700
New Berlin WI 53151
414 784 6880

Andrews Nelson Whitehead
31-10 48th Avenue
Long Island City NY 11101
718 937 7100

Amsterdam Art
1013 University Avenue
Berkeley CA 94710
415 548 9663

Color Craft
14 Airport Park Road
E. Granby CT 06026
800 243 2712

Earth Guild
33 Haywood Street
Asheville NC 28801
800 327 8448

SOUTH AFRICA

X-Press Graph-X
29 Siemert Road
Doornfontein
011 402 4522

Crafty Supplies
32 Main Road
Claremont
Cape
021 610 286

AUSTRALIA

Janet's Art Books Pty Ltd
143 Victoria Avenue
Chatswood NSW 2067
02 417 8572

Handworks Supplies
121 Commercial Road
South Yarra VOC 3141
03 820 8399

NEW ZEALAND

Gordon Harris
4 Gillies Avenue
Newmarket
Auckland
520 4466

Littlejohns
170 Victoria Street
Wellington
385 2099

Acknowledgements

Thanks to the following for generously donating materials or allowing us to borrow props for use in the photographic shoots: Absolutely; Catherine Nimmo; Celia Birtwell; Designers Guild; Global Village; Graham and Green; Harwood Antiques; Helen Baide; Kipp Flowers; Nomad; The Chelsea Gardener; The Dining Room Shop; The Kabah; The Nursery; Tobias and the Angel.

Index

Use these outlines for the Stripy Fish
Magnets (p.24), or trace others from
books, if you prefer, perhaps
including an octopus and a seahorse
for variety. Do not trace the stripes, as
your outlines will be covered with
pulp and so the lines will not show;
they are here for guidance for
decoration only.

The 8-pointed star is for the Starry Napkin Rings (p.28). The shaded areas are painted gold and the unshaded area filled in with yellow crayon.

The sun, flower and birds are to decorate the Mexican Mirror (p.32). Trace the designs and mark them along the border, so that a flower falls in the centre of the top and bottom panels, a bird in the centre of the side panels and a sun at each corner.

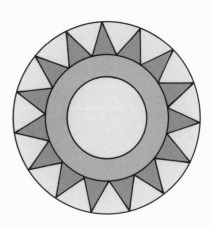

You will need 6 of these sunflowers to complete the Sunflower Bowl (p.36). Trace the design and transfer it so that the flowers are evenly spaced. Inserting carbon paper between the design and the bowl, and then drawing over the design, is probably the easiest way of transferring a design repeatedly like this. As in the case of the star (above), the shaded areas are painted gold and the unshaded areas are filled in with yellow crayon.

This central motif for the Sunflower Bowl (p.36) is the correct size to accompany the sunflowers opposite. The outer rim and alternate triangles and stars are coloured in red; the intervening triangles and diamonds are in green; the starry band and inner rim are in yellow, and the remaining stars match the Prussian blue of the bowl. Use liquid gold to surround the triangles. A green and white band completes the design.

These Roman numerals make a striking decoration for a large bowl. In the photograph on p.36, the numerals have been coloured alternately yellow and gold, with coloured triangles in between. The central motif is a floral variation on that of the Sunflower Bowl.

Use this irregular star template to cut pairs of stars for each Twinkling Star (p.44) you wish to make. The central hole is where the mirror will glint through. The swirly shapes mark the position and form of the interior wall filler decoration.

This double handle sits atop a variation on the Musical Box, as shown on pp. 19 and 56. If your scalpel slips when you are cutting, and the two parts get separated, use masking tape to join them.

V

The handle on the left is for the Seashore Urn (p.48). Trace this shape and transfer it on to some strong card, then reverse the tracing and repeat the process to get a mirror image handle for the other side of the urn. The handle on the right is for the Gilded Bowl (p.52) and the Musical Box (p.56). For each you will need to cut two, as above.

The animals shown here and on
p. VIII are for the Farmyard Mobile
(p.62). You can, of course, add other
animals of your own design, or change
from the farmyard theme to, for
example, a jungle one – with a tiger,
lion, monkey, elephant and giraffe.

As an alternative to animals, you could make a sea-life mobile instead. Use the fish shapes provided on p.I and the one above, and perhaps add some other forms of aquatic life. If you prefer, use these templates to make animal magnets instead, following the instructions on pp.26-7.

These are the component parts of the daisies shown on p.66. The petals (left) are stuck into the tops of the flower stems in an irregular fashion (see the flower-head, above). The leaves (far left) are also irregular. The stems of the flowers and leaves are strengthened by the wires being twisted together. The covering layers of paper strips give them their final shape (shown here).

This outline of the Shepherd's Clock (p.74) is shown for guidance only. All the measurements for making the clock

shape are provided on p.75. You may find another pair of hands useful when taping the card pieces together.

 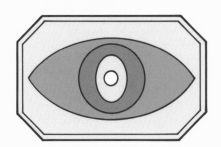

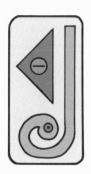 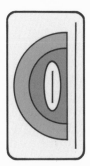 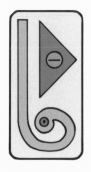 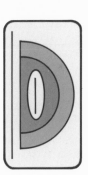

The design shown top left is for the Brilliant Brooch (p.80). The other designs are all variations that you could use for brooches. The sets of smaller designs at the bottom are for earrings. Many of the other motifs reproduced in this template section would also make charming brooch shapes to be decorated: for example, the sunflower or star from p.II, not to mention the fish (p.I) and the farm animals (pp.VII-VIII).

This design provides the rim shape and decoration for the Star-rimmed Bowl (p.86).

Trace the rim shape, turn your tracing paper round, and trace again to complete the circle. The layout of the decoration is for guidance only.